ICONS

KRAZY KIDS' FOOD!

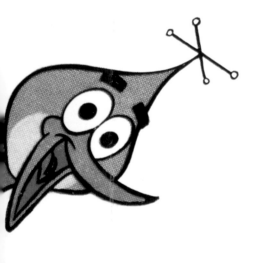

AUDREY.

MERRY christmas '03

KRAZY KIDS' FOOD!

Ed. Steve Roden and Dan Goodsell

Introduction by
Steve Roden

TASCHEN

KÖLN LONDON LOS ANGELES MADRID PARIS TOKYO

Front cover:
Eat It All Ice Cream Cones sign, 1960s
Back cover:
Frosted Flakes cereal box detail, 1955
Endpapers:
Post Alpha-Bits Cereal, 1950s;
Lucky Charms Cereal, 1960s

© 2003 TASCHEN GmbH
Hohenzollernring 53, D–50672 Köln
www.taschen.com

Editorial Coordination: Dan Goodsell & Steve Roden
Design: Adrienne Wong, Double Happiness Design, New York
Photos by: Artworks, Pasadena
Production: Tina Ciborowius, Cologne
Project management: Sonja Altmeppen, Cologne
English-language editor: Jim Heimann, Los Angeles
German translation: Harald Hellmann, Cologne
French translation: Simone Manceau, Paris

Printed in Italy
ISBN 3–8228–2237–X

KRAZY KIDS' FOOD!

Sugar coated memories:
Krazy Kids' Food!

In 1935, Post cereals licensed the rights to a popular new movie character, Mickey Mouse, and thus the marketing of kids' food changed forever. Mickey was placed prominently on Post Toasties cereal boxes and sales soared. Other manufacturers jumped on the character marketing bandwagon and the kids' food business as a whole took off. Throughout the 1940s and early 1950s movie and comic book characters were licensed to appear on packages of cereal, cookies, and candy. Companies raced to create new identities for themselves by marrying their products to existing characters such as the Lone Ranger, whose blazing guns appeared on the

fronts of Cheerios boxes. Disney used their stable of characters, including Donald Duck, to promote everything from bread to chocolate syrup. Characters from the Sunday funnies, such as Dick Tracy and Prince Valiant, got their faces on the fronts of candy boxes. Some companies even began to create new products specifically marketed to kids, including Popeye-shaped macaroni and cookies based on the popular Christmas character Rudolph the Red-Nosed Reindeer.

In the mid-1950s the first black-and-white animated television commercials were produced, and marketing strategies changed again. Licensing of existing characters was becoming expensive, so many food companies turned to ad agencies. The agencies designed the first generation of animated characters specifically intended to sell things to kids via television. The Spoonmen came from outer space and landed on the front of spoon-size Shredded Wheat boxes; while Marky Maypo screamed "I want my Maypo" on TV sets across the country. Children mimicked his cry and moms everywhere were forced to buy the oat cereal for their screaming kids.

The 1960s turned out to be the golden age of kids' food. As the "modern" world became more hectic, new products were created to make meals faster and easier. Pop-Tarts were an instant hot breakfast from the toaster, Fizzies tablets made water into soda, and a box of Kreme Krunch cereal contained chunks of freeze-dried ice cream. As the products got crazier, so did the characters that pitched them. Quisp the "quazy" alien had his own cereal from Quaker, while Pillsbury created talking fruit characters such as Goofy Grape and Choo Choo Cherry for its Funny Face

instant drink mix packets. Animated cartoon characters also had their share of the limelight. The enormously popular prime-time cartoon family, the Flint-stones, appeared on candy, bubble bath, vitamins, and cereal boxes. The 1960s also left a legacy of characters still in existence today, such as Cap'n Crunch and Poppin' Fresh, the Pillsbury Doughboy; and recognizing the temper of the times, caricatures of "10 Little Indians," Frito Bandito, and buck-tooth Chinese men were all still considered acceptable to sell to kids.

As the 1970s rolled around, oddball products like Koogle, a flavored peanut butter spread, hit the shelves with its pitchman – a three-eyed monster who sang like Satchmo. The Freakies were a family of monsters who lived in a "freakie tree", and Ralston produced a cereal of the same name. After Hollywood gave Willy Wonka his own movie, Quaker turned him into an animated character promoting his own line of candy. Now that man had actually landed on the moon, advertisers could use the reality of space travel as a new marketing tool. In the 1950s, companies had hawked outer space via cartoon aliens and comic book imagery of space-helmeted kids zooming away from earth. The 1970s brought us Space Food Sticks, a kids' food product from Pillsbury that had originally been developed for real US astronauts.

All of the items pictured in this book were meant to have a very short life span – to appear on the grocery store shelves, get sold and eaten, and then the packaging was meant to be thrown away. For over fifteen years we have collected thousands of products. This book is a small sampling of the items produced from the 1930s up to the 1970s. Everyone has different memories of childhood; hopefully you will find some of the products you enjoyed and a few you wished your mom would have bought for you.

Left: supermarket interior, 1960s; *above*: supermarket checkout, 1960s; *below*: Eat It All Ice Cream Cones sign, 1960s

Zuckersüße Erinnerungen:
Krazy Kids' Food!

1935 sicherte sich der Frühstücksflockenhersteller Post die Verwertungsrechte an einer populären neuen Zeichentrickfigur namens Micky Maus und veränderte so das Marketing für Kinderlebensmittel, Kids' Food, für immer. Micky prangte auf den Kartons mit Post-Toasties-Flakes, und die Absatzzahlen schossen in die Höhe. Andere Hersteller griffen die Idee auf. Ein florierender Industriezweig entstand.

In den 40er und frühen 50er Jahren wurden Film- und Comic-Helden lizenziert, um auf den Verpackungen von Frühstücksflocken, Keksen und

Süßigkeiten zu erscheinen. Die Firmen wetteiferten um ein neues Produktimage. Disneys Comiccharaktere wurden auf breiter Front eingesetzt. Aber auch die Helden von den Comicseiten der Sonntagszeitungen, Figuren wie Dick Tracy oder Prinz Eisenherz, fanden sich auf Verpackungen wieder. Bald gab es sogar Makkaroni in Gestalt von Popeye oder Kekse, die sich das beliebteste Rentier der Welt, Rudolf Rotnase, zum Vorbild nahmen.

Mitte der 50er entstanden die ersten Schwarz-Weiß-Werbespots fürs Fernsehen und die Marketingstrategie änderte sich erneut. Die Lizenzen für bereits existierende Charaktere der Populärkultur wurden zunehmend kostspieliger und so wandten sich viele Lebensmittelproduzenten Hilfe suchend an Werbeagenturen. Diese entwarfen die erste Generation von Zeichentrickfiguren, die einzig dafür geschaffen waren, Kunde Kind via TV zu erreichen. Die Spoonmen kamen aus dem Weltall und landeten auf den löffelförmigen Packungen von Shredded Wheat, während Marky Maypo aus allen Fernsehapparaten lautstark forderte: „I want my Maypo!" Die Kinder griffen diesen Kampfruf begeistert auf und zwangen ihre entnervten Mütter, ihnen diese Frühstücksflocken zu kaufen.

Die 60er Jahre sollten zum goldenen Zeitalter von Kids' Food werden. Ganz im Stile einer zunehmend hektischen, modernen Welt brachte man Produkte auf den Markt, die sich rasch und problemlos verzehren ließen. Pop-Tarts waren Fruchttaschen, die man im Toaster aufbacken konnte, Fizzies Tabletten, die fades Leitungswasser in Limonade verwandelten, und eine Schachtel Kreme Krunch enthielt gefriergetrocknete Eiscremestückchen. Die Produkte wurden immer verrückter, und ihre Werbebotschafter standen ihnen in nichts nach. Quisp, der „quazy" Außerirdische

FRUIT Drinks

MADE FROM GENERAL MILLS FRUIT DRINK CONCENTRATES

warb für Flakes der Firma Quaker, während Pillsbury sprechende Früchte wie Goofy Grape und Choo Choo Cherry für ihre Funny-Face-Brausetütchen erfand. Auch Zeichentrickfiguren standen im Rampenlicht der Werbewirtschaft. Familie Feuerstein fand man schon kurz nach ihrem TV-Debut auf den Verpackungen von Süßigkeiten, Schaumbädern oder Vitaminpräparaten. Manche Charaktere aus den 60ern wie Cap'n Crunch oder Poppin' Fresh existieren noch heute; die „10 kleinen Negerlein" oder Chinesen mit vorstehenden Zähnen hingegen sind schon lange nicht mehr witzig.

Die 70er brachten keine großen Veränderungen. Ein so verrücktes Produkt wie Koogle, aromatisierte Erdnussbutter, hatte ein vieläugiges Monster als Werbemaskottchen, das wie Satchmo sang. Die Freakies waren eine Familie von Monstern, die in einem Baum wohnten und der Firma Ralston halfen, gleichnamige Cerealien zu verkaufen. Und nachdem der Mensch tatsächlich auf dem Mond gelandet war, konnten die Werbestrategen auch den nun Wirklichkeit gewordenen Menschheitstraum für ihre Zwecke nutzen. Hatten sie in den 50ern Aliens und Kids mit Raumfahrerhelmen noch durch ein Comicweltall fliegen lassen, so tischten sie uns in den 70ern Space Food Sticks auf, ein Kinderlebensmittel der Firma Pillsbury, das ursprünglich für die amerikanischen Astronauten entwickelt worden war.

All den Produkten, die Sie in diesem Buch finden, war eigentlich nur eine kurze Lebensspanne zugedacht: Sie tauchten in den Regalen der Lebensmittelgeschäfte auf, wurden verkauft und konsumiert, und die Verpackungen sollten im Müll landen. Über mehr als 15 Jahre haben wir tausende von Kids'-Food-Artikeln zusammengetragen. Dieses Buch zeigt eine kleine Auswahl aus den 30er bis 70er Jahren, Zeugnisse einer Populärkultur, die sich ins kollektive Gedächtnis der amerikanischen Konsumenten eingeprägt hat. Aber vielleicht entdecken auch Sie ein Produkt, auf das Sie als Kind ganz verrückt gewesen wären.

Left: Donald Duck bread sign, 1950s; *above:* General Mills fruit drink sign, 1960s; *below:* Tinkerbell bread display, 1950s.

Souvenirs sucrés :
Krazy Kids' Food!

En 1935, les céréales Post acquièrent les droits pour un nouveau personnage de cinéma : Mickey. Fini le marketing traditionnel des aliments pour enfant – kids' food –, il suffit que Mickey s'affiche sur les paquets de céréales Post Toasties, pour que les ventes décollent. Les

autres fabricants suivent et, au cours des années 40 et au début des années 50, tous les personnages de films et de bandes dessinées sont brevetés pour venir faire de la figuration sur les paquets de céréales, de biscuits et autres confiseries. Les compagnies se créent une image en mariant leurs produits à des personnages existants. Ainsi, Lone Ranger le cow-boy ne tarde pas à apparaître sur les boîtes de Cheerios. Disney met tous ses personnages à contribution afin de promouvoir des produits allant du pain au sirop de chocolat. On retrouve sur les boîtes de bonbons les visages de héros des B.D. dominicales, tels Dick Tracy ou Prince Vaillant. Quelques compagnies créent même des produits destinés aux petits, comme des macaronis en forme de Popeye ou des biscuits inspirés de Rudolph, le renne au nez rouge, qui conduit le traîneau du père Noël.

Above: Ping the Pixie candy box, 1950s; *top right:* Freakies cereal, 1974; *below right:* Galaxy syrup bottle, 1950s.

Au milieu des années 50, les premiers spots publicitaires en noir et blanc sont produits pour la télévision, ce qui entraîne à nouveau un changement des stratégies de vente. L'exploitation de personnages existants devenant onéreuse, nombre de compagnies se tournent vers des agences publicitaires qui créent alors la première génération de personnages animés, conçus pour vendre des produits destinés aux enfants, par le biais de la télévision. Les Spoonmen venus de l'espace atterrissent sur les paquets de céréales Shredded Wheat, tandis que Marky Maypo clame « Je veux mon Maypo » sur tous les petits écrans du pays. Les enfants l'imitent et, partout, les mamans courent acheter le produit.

Les années 60 seront l'âge d'or de l'alimentation pour enfants. À mesure que le monde s'accélère, on a de moins en moins le temps et l'envie de préparer les repas. Les Pop-Tarts proposent un petit déjeuner instantané, jailli du grille-pain. Les comprimés Fizzies transforment l'eau en soda, et les paquets de céréales Kreme Krunch abritent de gros morceaux de crème glacée lyophilisée. Plus les produits deviennent fous, plus les personnages sont comiques. L'étrange Quisp possède sa propre

céréale chez Quaker, Pillsbury invente des fruits parlants, tels le raisin Goofy et la cerise Choo Choo pour Funny Face, sa gamme de boissons instantanées. Les personnages de dessins animés ne sont pas en reste. La famille Pierrafeu fait son apparition sur les boîtes de bonbons, de sels de bain, de vitamines et de céréales. Il nous reste des années 60 toute une galerie de personnages, tels Cap'n Crunch, Poppin' Fresh ou Pillsbury Doughboy. Témoignage de l'air du temps, les Dix Petits Indiens, Frito le Bandito ou les Chinois aux dents en avant, étaient considérés comme parfaitement acceptables.

Pas de changement notable au cours des années 70. Des produits incongrus comme Koogle, le beurre de cacahuète aromatisé, remportent un succès foudroyant avec un monstre à trois yeux qui chante avec la voix de Satchmo. Les monstres Freakies vivent dans un arbre aussi bizarre qu'eux, et Ralston produit une céréale éponyme. Quand Hollywood consacre un film à Willy Wonka, Quaker le transforme en un personnage animé, pour promouvoir sa propre ligne de confiseries. Et quand l'homme marche sur la lune, les annonceurs ont un nouvel outil de vente. Si les années 50 avaient leurs extraterrestres de dessins animés et des bandes dessinées montrant des gamins en tenue spatiale et s'envolant comme des fusées, les années 70 apportent les Bâtonnets alimentaires pour l'Espace, un produit de Pillsbury destiné aux enfants, mais développé au départ pour les astronautes américains.

A peine apparus sur les étagères des épiceries, tous les articles figurant dans ce livre étaient vendus, engloutis, et leur emballage jeté à la poubelle. Nous en avons récupéré des milliers en plus de quinze ans. Ce livre est un échantillonnage des produits commercialisés entre les années 30 et 70. Espérons que vous y retrouverez le goût de votre enfance.

Mickey Mouse Cookies, 1930s
Disney Post cereals display, 1930s

HAVE YOU SEEN THE MARVELOUS

MICKEY MOUSE

or other Walt Disney

CUT-OUTS

on all Post Toasties boxes!

HERE'S lots of fun for boys and girls! Mickey Mouse and his pals — Minnie Mouse, Pluto the Pup, Horace Horse-collar, or the Goof — on some Post Toasties boxes! And on other boxes the Three Little Pigs and the Big Bad Wolf.

What fun they are! And how much fun to eat Post Toasties, too — the delicious, crispy cereal that stays so nice and crunchy in milk or cream! The whole family will love Post Toasties . . . especially with fruits or berries!

But make sure mother gets you real Post Toasties . . . the only cereal with these marvelous toys for you — absolutely free! Post Toasties is a product of General Foods.

By special arrangement with Walt Disney Enterprises © 1934

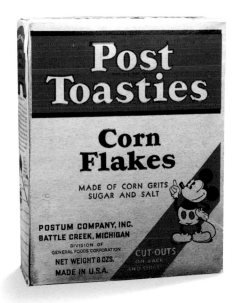

Mickey Mouse Post cereals ad, 1934
Mickey Mouse Post Toasties cereal box, 1935

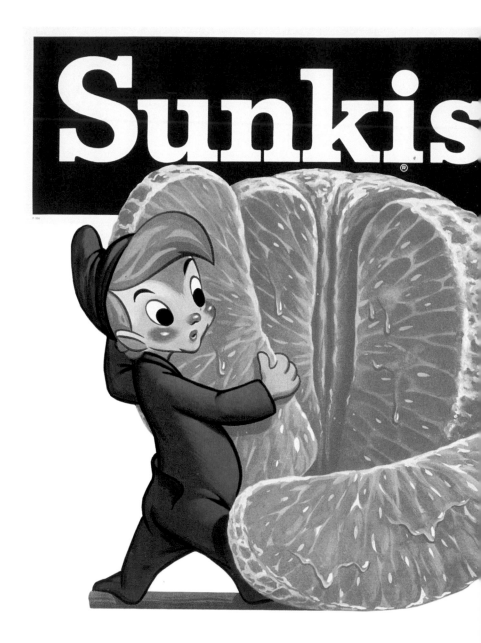

Disney Sunkist oranges sign, 1960s
Donald Duck Chocolate Syrup can, 1950s

nald duck

1-FROST

FROZEN FUD

OR SWELL G

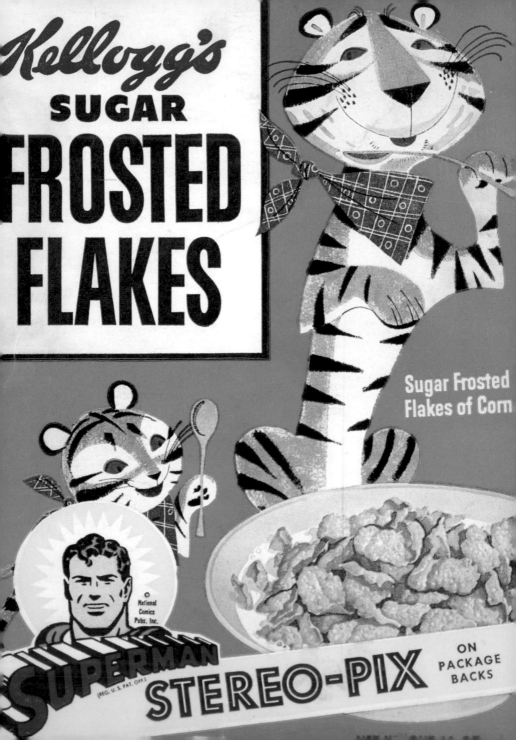

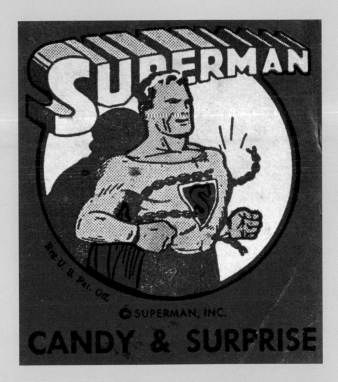

Superman Frosted Flakes cereal box, 1955
Superman candy box, 1940
Previous page: Donald Duck Fudgi-Frost sign, 1956

Dick Tracy and Joe Palooka candy boxes, 1950s
Popeye Buitoni macaroni box, 1950s

BUITONI

SAY BUITONI—AS IN BEAUTY

POPEYE

ENRICHED
SPINACH MACARONI PRODUCT

CONTAINS
20%
PROTEIN

*DEFATTED
WHEAT GERM
AND
FOOD YEAST
ADDED!*

FREE!
NEW, EXCITING
TOY
IN EVERY
BOX!

REPLACEMENT OR REFUND OF
Guaranteed by
Good Housekeeping

HEY KIDS! Join the BIG
Post Cereals' Roundup!
©WM. BOYD
Get
HOPPY'S
36 WILD WES
TRADING CARDS
FREE
OF EXTRA COST!
There's a Hopalong Cassidy Wild West Trading Card for
in every box of these chuck-wagon favorites. No money-
boxtops needed! Get 'em at Mom's favorite grocer's—in
Post Cereal boxes marked "WILD WEST TRADING CAR
These are mighty fine trading cards! On one side they're decorated with full-color pictures of Wild West scenes. And on the other side there's Hoppy's own personal picture plus an exciting description of the scene on the front of the card. Look—here
are just a few of the grand
you get in the complete assort
of thirty-six: "Hoppy Shoo
Rattlesnake," "Hoppy F
Gold," "Fancy Rope Spinni
Be the first member of your
to have a complete set of 36!
Trade 'em! Collect 'em! Round up the whole set!
Post TOASTIES Corn Flakes
POST TOASTIES ...THEY'RE HEAP GOOD CORN FLAKES, HONEST INJUN!
Post's GRAPE-NUTS FLAKES
HOPALONG CASSIDY WILD WEST
GRAND-TASTIN' POST'S GRAPE-NUTS FLAKES HAVE THAT SPECIAL SUGAROASTED FLAVOR!
Post's 40% BRAN FLAKES
HOPALONG CASSIDY WILD WEST TRADING CARD IN THIS PACKAGE!
MOM AND POP ARE MIGHTY WISE...THEY KNOW POST'S 40% BRAN FLAKES ARE GOOD... AND GOOD FOR 'EM!
NEW-No Sugar Needed! Post's SUGAR CRISP
Candy-coated Puffed Wheat
NEW POST'S SUGAR CRISP...AS A EREAL IT'S DANDY OR EAT IT LIKE CANDY!
Post's RAISIN BRAN
HOPALONG CASSIDY WILD WEST TRADING CARD IN THIS PACKAGE!
EVERYBODY LOVES POST'S RAISIN BRAN ...THE FRUIT 'N CEREAL COMBINATION THAT'S HARD TO BEAT!
Products of General Foods
FREE
NOW I'VE GOT ALL 36 CARDS

Hopalong Cassidy Post cereals ad, 1951
Hopalong Cassidy Cookies box, 1950

Lone Ranger Cheerios cereal box, 1948
Sky King Cookies box, 1950s

ABISC
SKY KING
Sky King
COOKIES
Y KING
SHERIFF
LOOK!
SKY KING PICTURE TO COLO
ON BACK OF PACKAGE!

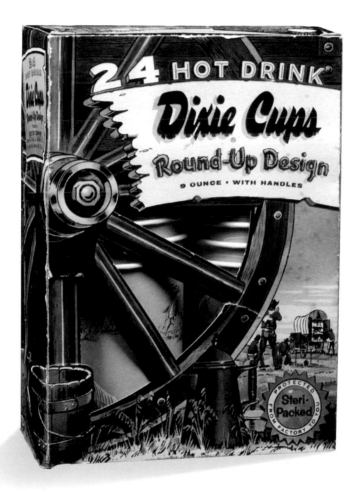

Rootie Kazootie Cookies box, 1950s
Western Dixie Cups box, 1950s

Farfel Nestlé soda sign, 1950s
Rudolph the Red-Nosed Reindeer Cookies box, 1950s

Burry's
SIMPLE SIMON
BRAN MUFFIN
MIX
NET WEIGHT 10
INGREDIENTS:
Wheat Flour, Bran, Sugar, Vegetable Sh
ening, Leavening, Molasses, Salt,

Simple Simon Bran Muffin Mix box, 1944
Hansel and Gretel Cookies box, 1950s

Brach's Rocket Mix box, 1950s
Rocket Rangers candy box, 1950s
Spacemen Buitoni macaroni box, 1950s

BUITONI

SAY BUITONI — AS IN BEAUTY

SPACE MEN

20% Protein Enriched
MACARONI
Highest in Protein
Lowest in Starch

OF ALL LEADING BRANDS TESTED

FREE!
A different, exciting
TOY
in every box!

NET WT
8 OZS.

REPLACEMENT OR REFUND OF MO...
Guaranteed by
Good Housekeeping
IF NOT AS ADVERTISED THEREIN

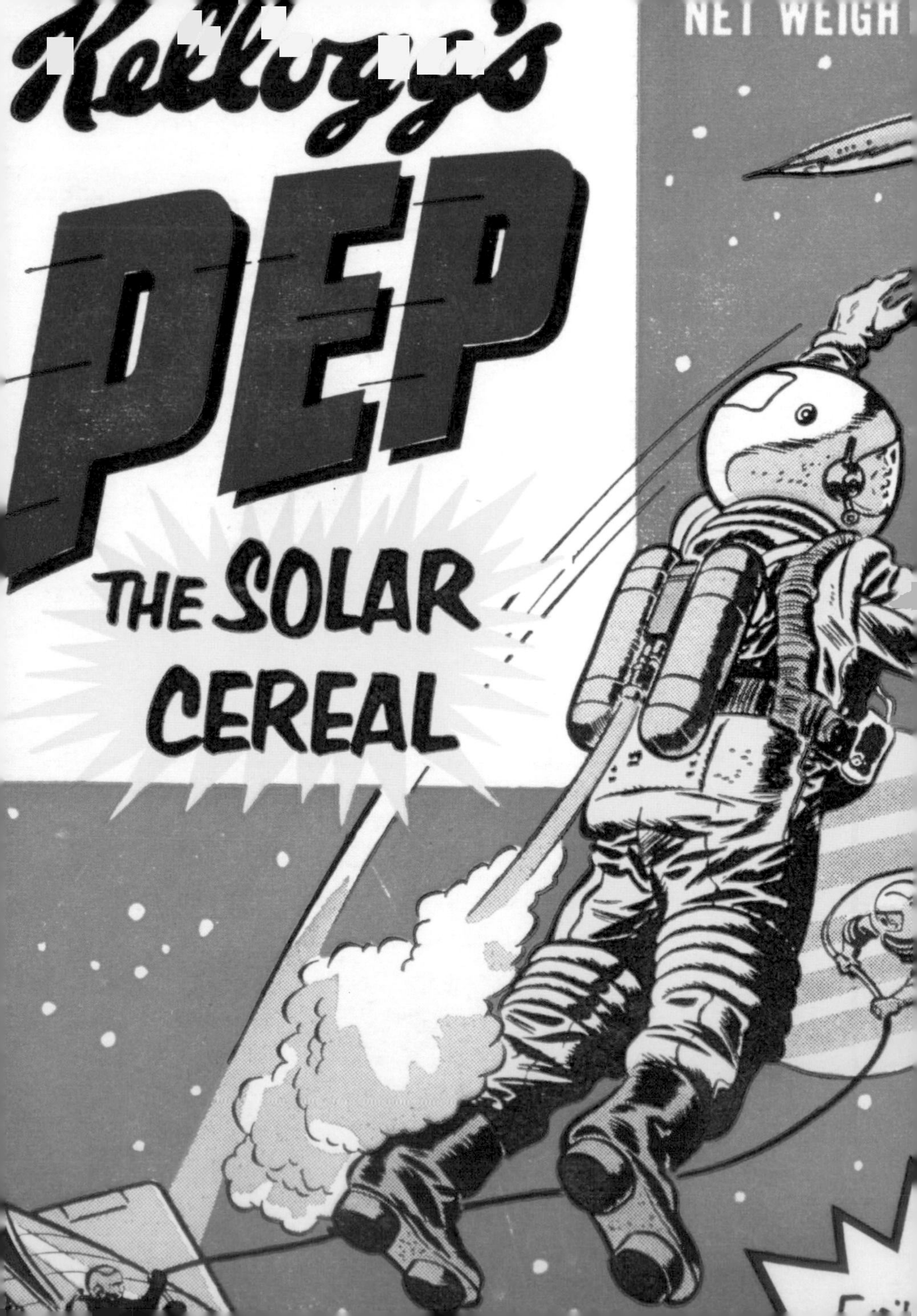
Kellogg's
PEP
THE SOLAR
CEREAL
NET WEIGH

Tom Corbett Pep cereal boxes, 1950s

Frankie Luer booklet, 1955
Popsicle Major Mars ad, 1952

Outer Space cups box, 1950s
Mr. Astro-Chimp Dairy Queen ad, 1961

Dairy Queen

presents MR. ASTRO-CHIMP*

WHAT A PLAYMATE! — Your youngsters will go into orbit when they see this funny fellow. He stands a full 22" high . . . almost life size! Mr. Astro-Chimp hangs by his hand, and holds a banana too. Made of finest quality plush and vinyl, he's comparable to chimps selling up to $6.98 retail.

Yours for only
$2.99
Includes Postage.
In Canada
Import Duty Extra.

WITH ORDER BLANK FROM YOUR DAIRY QUEEN STORE
Limited time only . . .
offer void after June 1st, 1961.

Enjoy these delicious taste treats at . . .

Dairy Queen

Malts & Shakes

Par-Fay Sundaes

Sundaes

. . . serving "the treat with the curl on top"* at more than 3,000 U. S. and Canadian stores

Straw Short

n Nat'l. Dev. Co.

Post Count Off cereal box, 1960s
Nabisco Spoonman cereal box, 1950s

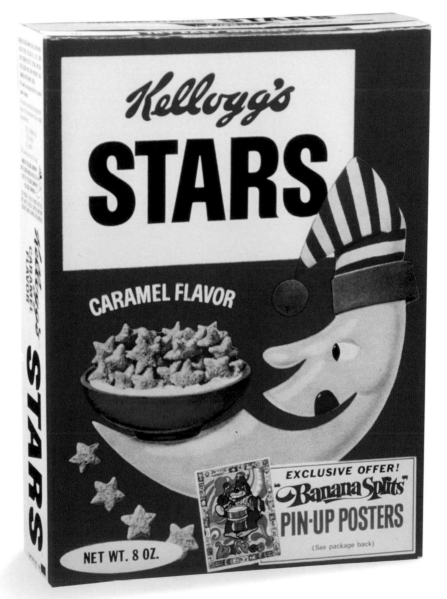

Stars cereal box, 1969
Jets cereal box, 1950s

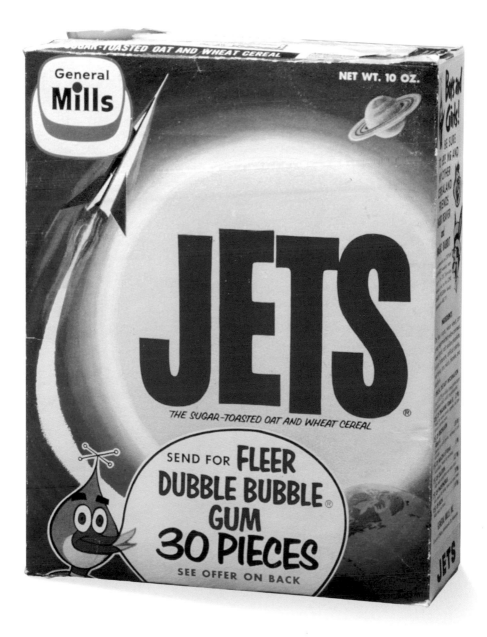

Clanky and Noom Chocolate Syrup containers, 1963 and 1966
Jet Pop popcorn container, 1964

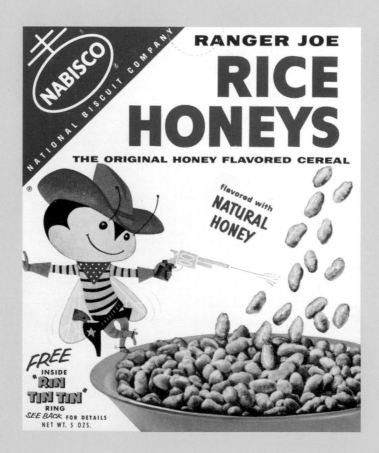

Rice Honeys cereal box, 1955
Bar-B-Q Potato Chips bag, 1950s

ircus Bath Soap!

I grow "fur"

PRINTED IN U.S.A.

FW2-206

Fuzzy Wuzzy Soap sign, 1966

Silly Soap containers, 1965
Matey bubble bath box, 1961

FREE TOY
WITH PURCHASE
25-30 BATHS PER BOX
mateY®
WITH LANOLIN AND HEXACHLOROPHENE
MMENDED BY THE CONSUMER SERVICE BUREAU OF ARENTS' MAGAZINE VERTISED THEREIN
PLEASE READ DIRECTIONS FOR USE ON SIDE OF BOX

Delicious new instant soft drink
discovery from Nestlé
it's Keen!

jar serves an army of kids for ½ the cost of bottled s
rinks without the bother of bottles. At your grocers no

TLE'S KEEN IN 5 YUMMY FLAVORS ■ JUST ADD WATER ■ SUGAR'S IN IT ■ NON-CARBONATED ■ VITAMIN C FORTIFI

Nestlé Keen ad, 1963
Sealtest Choo Choo Chocolate ice cream box, 1960s

Fizzies drink tablets, 1950s
Flex-Straw box, 1960s
Dip 'n Sip box, 1960s

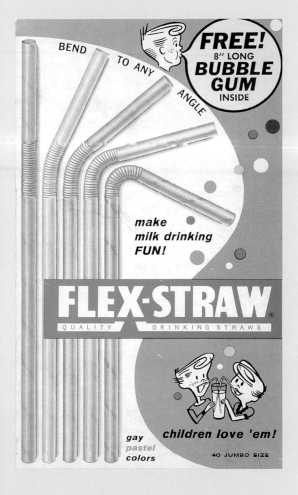

Kellogg's STRAWBERRY
KREAM KRUNCH

Chunks of
REAL ICE CREAM
Freeze-dried in a
nutritious cereal

NET WT. 6 OZ.

Kream Krunch cereal box, 1965
Carnation and Big Deal ice cream boxes, 1960s

Cola Bear bottle, 1960s
Tiger Shake box, 1963

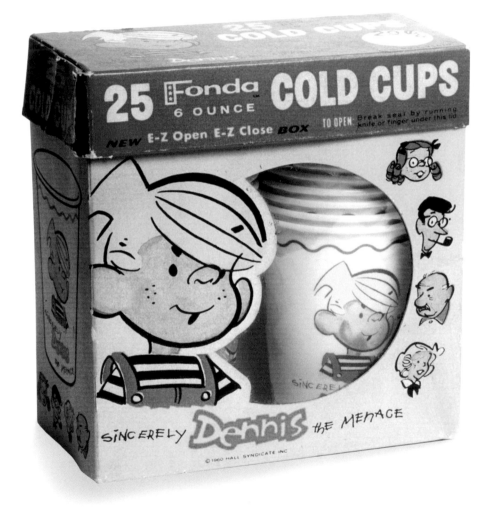

Dennis the Menace Cups box, 1960
Bugs Bunny Cups box, 1959

Beatles Yeah Yeah candy boxes, 1960s

♪ BRUSHA...BRUSHA...
GET THE NEW
IT'S DANDY FOR Y

Bucky B

♪ ♫
USHA
NA —
TEETH!
er

Mr. Bubble containers, 1970s
Bucky Beaver Ipana toothpaste ad, 1950s

Crazy Foam containers, 1960s

Scout Cookie

Me is Here...

p us with our

ps this year!

COOKIES

1912
50th
Anniversary

Wild Cherry, Black Jack and Grape gum, 1960s
Sealtest chocolate milk carton, 1960s
Previous page: Girl Scout Cookies sign, 1962

Toucan Sam Froot Loops sign, 1963
Corn Flakes with Bananas cereal box, 1964

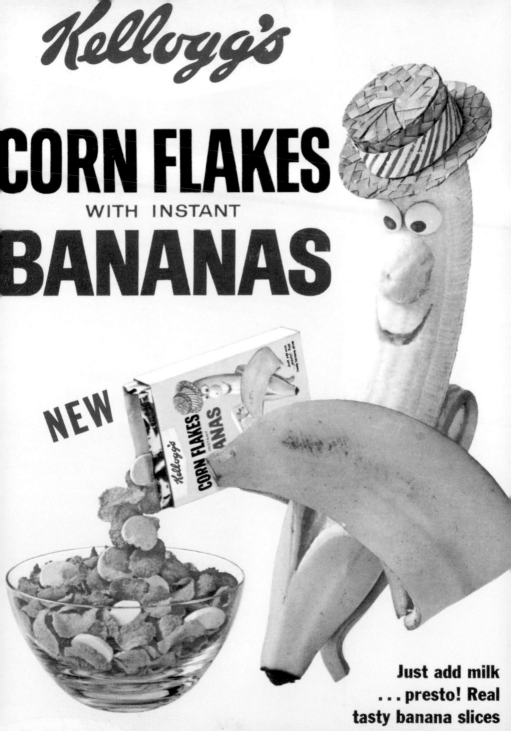

Turtle Tangerine Drink-Aid package, 1960s
Jif Peanut Butter jar, 1950s

Big Shot chocolate syrup, 1963
King Stir drink wands, 1960s

Dubble Bubble gum box, 1960s
Bazooka and Dubble Bubble gum, 1960s

Mr. Chips cookies box, 1960s
Maypo cereal box, 1956

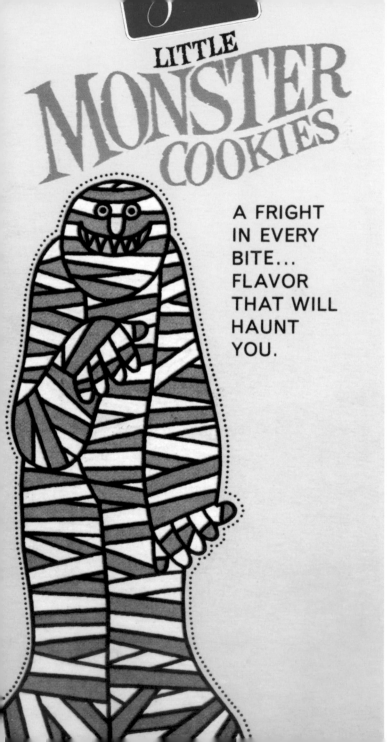

LITTLE MONSTER COOKIES

A FRIGHT
IN EVERY
BITE...
FLAVOR
THAT WILL
HAUNT
YOU.

Little Monster Cookies box, 1960s
Trick or Treat Candy box, 1950s
Tricks or Treats Cookies box, 1956

Devil Gum box, 1960
Brach's Halloween candy sign, 1966

The Phantom candy box, 1960s
Strictly Fun Monster candy boxes, 1960s

Yogi Bear Corn Flakes sign, 1960s
Huckleberry Hound Corn Flakes sign, 1961

Felix the CAT

ELIX THE CAT
ROD. Inc.

Felix the Cat candy box, 1960s
The Jetsons candy boxes, 1960s

Flintstones candy boxes, 1960s

Flintstones Vitamins, 1969
Flintstones bubble bath box, 1965

Space Ghost bubble bath box, 1967
Gigantor bubble bath container, 1964

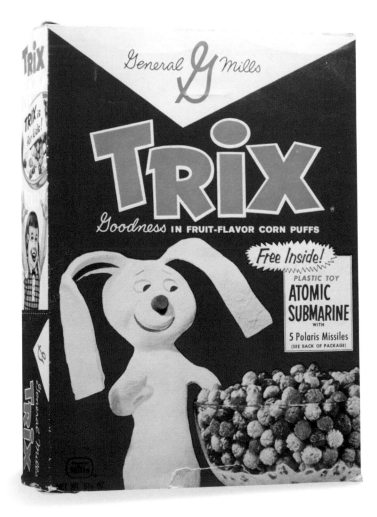

Trix cereal box, 1950s
Triple Snack cereal box, 1963

Cocoa Krispies cereal photo, 1960s
Cocoa Puffs cereal box, 1950s

Katy Kangaroo Frosted Flakes display, 1952
FrostyO's cereal box, 1960s

Pop-Tarts box, 1964
Milton the Toaster sign, 1970s

w SPAGHETTIC
18 little meatba

new spaghetti you can eat with a sp

American brought you spoonable SpaghettiOs. And now hold on
cause SpaghettiOs with meatballs is here! Rollicking spaghetti
eefy little meatballs in a bright tomato sauce. So easy to handl
vention since the napkin. Makes a meaty meal in minutes. Try

7¢.

Del Monte fruit drink can, 1966
Libby's fruit drink cans, 1960s
Previous page: SpaghettiOs ad, 1966

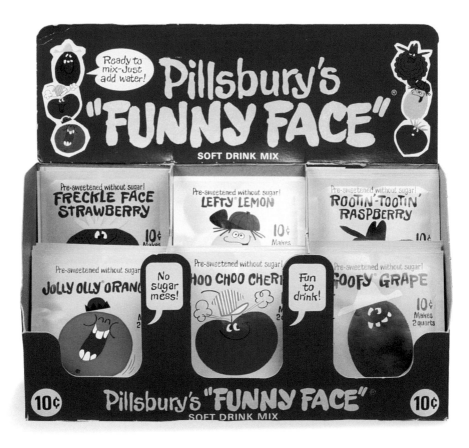

Funny Face display box, 1966
Wrapples package, 1977

OW!
Fresh Caramel Apples...Quick & Easy
Wrapple
neat
heets of Caramel
ith sticks for making
Caramel Apples
from
KRAFT
T WT. 9 OZS. · 6 CARAMEL SHEETS · 6 FREE STICKS
(255 g)
NT PENDING
Best when purchased by
APR-9-77
V 4

"FUNN

Mr. Wiggle Jell-O boxes, 1966
Previous page: Funny Face sign, 1960s

Pillsbury Doughboy cupcake mix box, 1970s
Life cereal ad, 1963

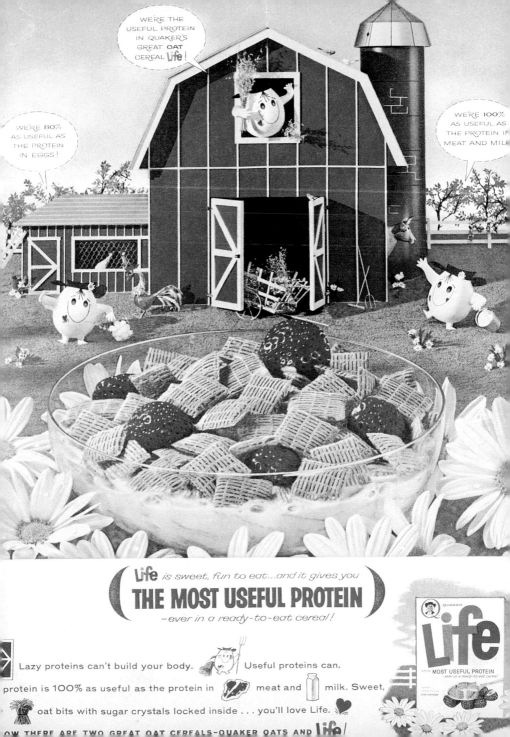

Shake-A Pudd'n box, 1967
Puddin' Head box, 1966

Tang jar, 1960s
Space Food Sticks box, 1970s

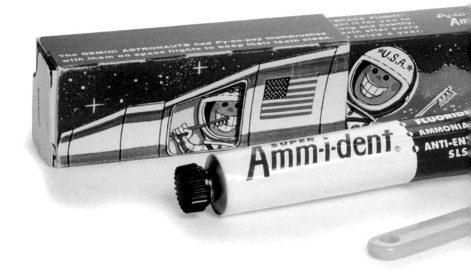

Amm-i-dent space toothpaste, 1960s
Dre's Space Tube Candy, 1965

Wheat Honeys cereal box, 1960s
Rice Honeys Spacemen cereal box, 1969

NABISCO
FREE
2 SPACE
EXPLORERS INSIDE
COLLECT ALL 6
ACTUAL SIZE
FROSTED WITH
GOLDEN
HONEY-FLAVORED
GLAZE
RICE
HONEYS

Chocolate Fudge and Strawberry Quik, 1960s
Chocolate Malted and Vanilla Quik, 1960s

12 SAFE-T CUPS

SAFE-T CUP

Fresh-kept IN A POLY BAG

WHAT BETTER FLAVOR!

GET 2 HANDY DIPPERS FOR ONLY $1.00 AND THIS BOX TOP!

Fresh when you buy them! Fresh when you serve them!

CRISPER IN A POLY BAG FOR GUARANTEED FRESHNESS

SAFE-T Cups & Cones

Safe-T Cups Cone box, 1960s
Adams ice cream gum packages, 1970s

Fun
to
make

JIFFY POP

JP-140K Printed in U.S.A.

Fun to eat!

9¢

POPCORN

Pals vitamins box, 1975
Nugget Town chocolate milk mix box, 1970s
Previous page: Jiffy Pop Monkey sign, 1960s

Zooper Dooper box, 1971
Life Savers Funhouse box, 1976
Fruit Stripe bubble gum box, 1970s

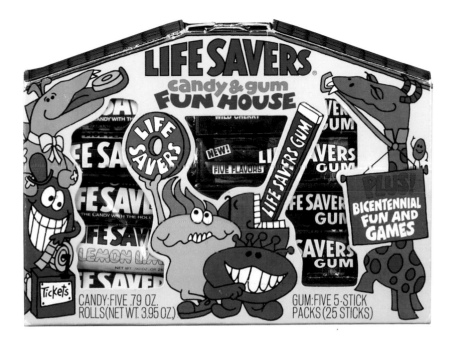

Fizzies drink tablets packets, 1960s

Paas Easter Egg Color Kits, 1960s

Puffa Puffa Rice cereal box, 1968
OGG Cocoa Krispies cereal box, 1969

Jiffy Pop Indian sign, 1960s
Frito Bandito sign, 1968

Rath 10 Little Indians Wiener package, 1971
Wampum Corn Chips box, 1960s

Rots O' Ruck candy box, 1960s
Dippy Canoes container, 1960s

Sgt. Toppit ice cream sprinkles, 1970s
Cap'n Crunch cereal box, 1963

NEW!
Tastes like
Oatmeal Cookies

Post
Oat Flakes

MADE WITH OAT, SOY, AND RICE FLOURS — DELICIOUSLY FLAVORED

10 OUNCES/*Net Wt. 284 Grams—K*

Oat Flakes cereal box, 1960s
Hostess Twinkies box, 1971
Hostess Big Wheels box, 1971

Lemon Snaps box, 1962
Zuzu Ginger Snaps box, 1962
Chocolate Snaps box, 1962

tasty little snack baskets!
CHEESE FLAVORED POKES
NEW SNACK
A product of
Kellogg's
of Battle Cree

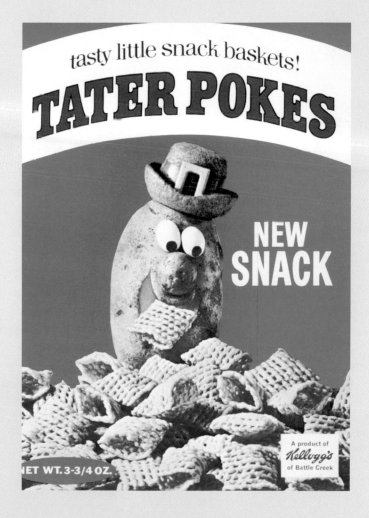

Cheese Pokes box, 1967
Tater Pokes box, 1967

Koogle Monster display, 1974
Koogle spread jar, 1974

Libbyland Sundown Supper box, 1971
Screaming Yellow Zonkers! box, 1970s

161

KER
SEND FOR M
CAVER
HELME
(see package back
NEW!
The Vitamin Powere
Sugary Cereal
quake
for EARTHQUAKE
power

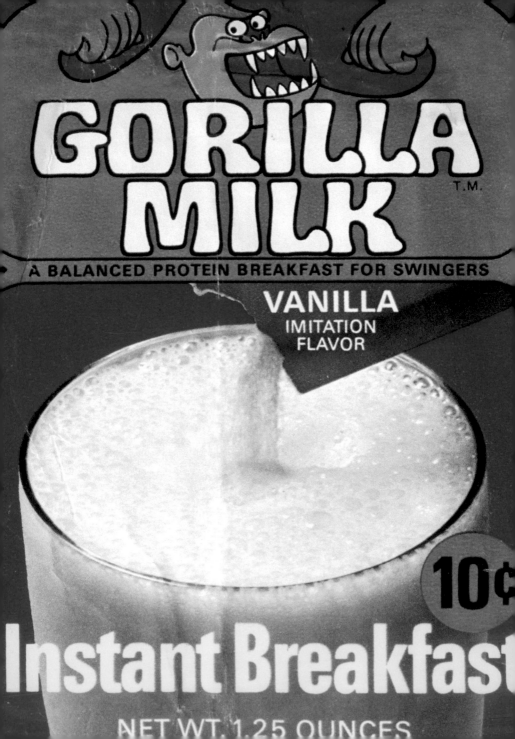

Gorilla Milk package, 1970s
Unicap elephant multivitamins, 1969
Previous pages: Quisp cereal box, 1969
Quake cereal box, 1967

Willy Wonka's Oompas candy, 1970s
Kool-Pops box, 1960s

TER CREME

LATY CREME

ANDY COATED

Kool·Pops ®

8 READY TO FREEZE PASTEURIZED POP BARS

HEY KIDS!
CIRCUS PUZZLE CARDS ON THE BACK

10 FL OZ
(296 mL) NET CONTENTS

Kool-Aid packages, 1970s

Oscar Mayer Wiener sign, 1960s
One A Day vitamins sign, 1960s

Popsicle Space-Shots sign, 1960s
Krypton Bubble Gum box, 1979

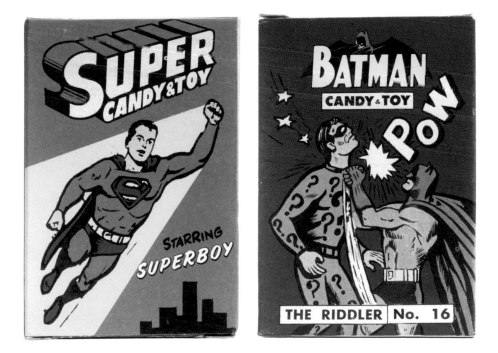

Superhero Candy boxes, 1966–67

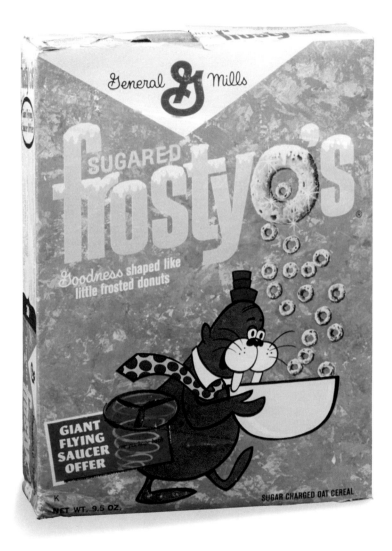

Pink Panther Flakes cereal box, 1970s
Chumley FrostyO's cereal box, 1960s

Fat Albert candy box, 1973
Jay Ward candy boxes, 1968

Spooky & Casper cookie box, 1968
Casper Sugar Chex cereal box, 1970

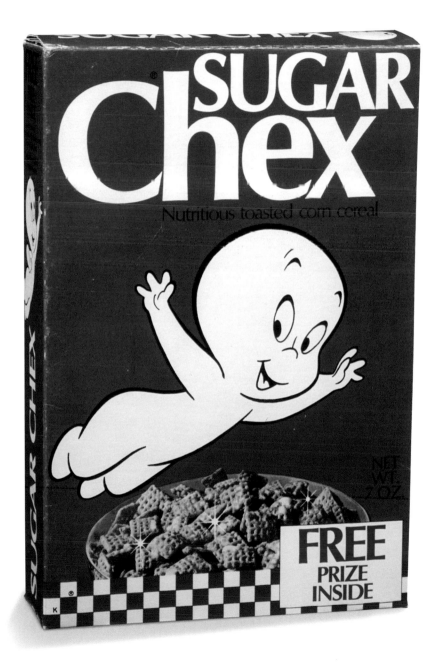

SUGAR Chex®
Nutritious toasted corn cereal

NET WT. 7 OZ.

FREE PRIZE INSIDE

SUGAR CHEX

Peanuts Weber's bread bag, 1971

Valentines candy boxes, 1960s
Love It's bubble gum box, 1970s
Previous pages: Bubble gum packages, 1970s

INSIST ON STAR BRITE BUBBLE GUM

REFRESHING

1¢ BIG BUBBLE

Ingredients: Sugar, Corn Syrup, Gum Base, Art. Flavors, Resinous Glaze, U.S. Cert'd. Food Color.
CRAMER GUM CO., INC., Boston 02128, U.S.A. — WORLD WIDE GUM CO., LTD., Granby, P.Q., Ca

UFO bubble gum card, 1960s
Pop Rocks candy package, 1970s

Razzles gum packages, 1969

Further information and photos of kids' food packaging can be found on our website: **http://theimaginaryworld.com**.

Dan Goodsell is an artist and collector living in Los Angeles, California. His collecting interests include kids' food packaging, amusement parks, and other aspects of popular culture. He has appeared on numerous collectibles TV shows. He maintains The Imaginary World website which showcases the authors' popular culture collections as well as his own theme park art project.

Steve Roden is a visual and sound artist living in Pasadena, California. For the last fifteen years he has spent major flea market hours with Dan Goodsell building the largest archive of original kids' food packaging in the world. He also collects ephemera, art, and objects related to modern architecture and design; and he has spent the last few years restoring Wallace Neff's 1946 experimental dome house. His artworks have been exhibited in museums and galleries internationally.

We would like to thank our friends and families and all the collectors and dealers in this field including Brian Razzi, Kevin and Lynn Burkett, Dennis Hasty, Dallas Poague, David Welch, Tod Machin, Scott Bruce, Robert Bruce, Sidney Sillick, Bernice Bauman, Joyce Kline, Joel Rassmussen, Randy and Kelly Jones, Jim and Linda Maley, John Krupienski, Ralph Stout, Bill Otto, Jim Rash, Jim Roselle, David Katz, David Gutterman, Jim Lambert, Roland Coover, Graham Trievel, Patrick Jenkins, Richard Kraft, Ron Faskowicz, Tim Krajewski, and Kevin Meisner. But most especially thanks to Sari and Shannon for putting up with endless hours of insignificant talk regarding kids' food and with the piles of packaging that fill our respective homes.

Adrienne Wong wishes to thank friends and family for all of their support: Kin Shaw, Diana, Stacey, and Colby Wong, Carolyn Wong, Diana Paiva, and Karin Spraggs-Hoyt — with special inspiration from Oliver and Malcolm Hoyt.

Special thanks to Jim Heimann, editor extraordinaire, and to Blue at Artworks, Pasadena, for the huge job of photographing the collection with special care and attention to all the small details.

All images are from the collection of Dan Goodsell and Steve Roden unless otherwise noted.

All-American Ads of the 40s
Ed. Jim Heimann
Flexi-cover, 768 pp.

All-American Ads of the 50s
Ed. Jim Heimann
Flexi-cover, 928 pp.

All-American Ads of the 60s
Ed. Jim Heimann
Flexi-cover, 960 pp.

"The ads do more than advertise products – they provide a record of American everyday life of a bygone era in a way that nothing else can." —*Associated Press*, USA

"Buy them all and add some pleasure to your life."

All-American Ads 40ˢ Ed. Jim Heimann	**Design of the 20ᵗʰ Century** Charlotte & Peter Fiell	**Future Perfect** Ed. Jim Heimann	**15ᵗʰ Century Paintings** Rose-Marie and Rainer Hagen	**Seba: Natural Curiosities** I. Müsch, R. Willmann, J. Rust
All-American Ads 50ˢ Ed. Jim Heimann	**Designing the 21ˢᵗ Century** Charlotte & Peter Fiell	**The Garden at Eichstätt** Basilius Besler	**16ᵗʰ Century Paintings** Rose-Marie and Rainer Hagen	**See the World** Ed. Jim Heimann
Angels Gilles Néret	**Dessous** Lingerie as Erotic Weapon Gilles Néret	**HR Giger** HR Giger	**Paris-Hollywood** Serge Jacques Ed. Gilles Néret	**Eric Stanton** Reunion in Ropes & Other Stories Ed. Burkhard Riemschneider
Architecture Now! Ed. Philip Jodidio	**Devils** Gilles Néret	**Indian Style** Ed. Angelika Taschen	**Penguin** Frans Lanting	**Eric Stanton** She Dominates All & Other Stories
Art Now Eds. Burkhard Riemschneider, Uta Grosenick	**Digital Beauties** Ed. Julius Wiedemann	**Kitchen Kitsch** Ed. Jim Heimann	**Photo Icons, Vol. I** Hans-Michael Koetzle	Ed. Burkhard Riemschneider
Atget's Paris Ed. Hans Christian Adam	**Robert Doisneau** Ed. Jean-Claude Gautrand	**Krazy Kids' Food** Eds. Steve Roden, Dan Goodsell	**Photo Icons, Vol. II** Hans-Michael Koetzle	**Tattoos** Ed. Henk Schiffmacher
Best of Bizarre Ed. Eric Kroll	**Eccentric Style** Ed. Angelika Taschen	**London Style** Ed. Angelika Taschen	**20ᵗʰ Century Photography** Museum Ludwig Cologne	**Edward Weston** Ed. Manfred Heiting
Bizarro Postcards Ed. Jim Heimann	**Encyclopaedia Anatomica** Museo La Specola, Florence	**Male Nudes** David Leddick	**Pin-Ups** Ed. Burkhard Riemschneider	
Karl Blossfeldt Ed. Hans Christian Adam	**Erotica 17ᵗʰ–18ᵗʰ Century** From Rembrandt to Fragonard Gilles Néret	**Man Ray** Ed. Manfred Heiting	**Giovanni Battista Piranesi** Luigi Ficacci	
California, Here I Come Ed. Jim Heimann	**Erotica 19ᵗʰ Century** From Courbet to Gauguin Gilles Néret	**Mexicana** Ed. Jim Heimann	**Provence Style** Ed. Angelika Taschen	
50ˢ Cars Ed. Jim Heimann		**Native Americans** Edward S. Curtis	**Pussy-Cats** Gilles Néret	
Chairs Charlotte & Peter Fiell	**Erotica 20ᵗʰ Century, Vol. I** From Rodin to Picasso Gilles Néret	Ed. Hans Christian Adam	**Redouté's Roses** Pierre-Joseph Redouté	
Classic Rock Covers Michael Ochs	**Erotica 20ᵗʰ Century, Vol. II** From Dalí to Crumb Gilles Néret	**New York Style** Ed. Angelika Taschen	**Robots and Spaceships** Ed. Teruhisa Kitahara	
Description of Egypt Ed. Gilles Néret		**Extra/Ordinary Objects, Vol. I** Ed. Colors Magazine	**Seaside Style** Ed. Angelika Taschen	

ICONS